BE A CARPENTER

GUIDE TO THE TRADES

Published in the United States of America by Cherry Lake Publishing
Ann Arbor, Michigan
www.cherrylakepublishing.com

Reading Adviser: Marla Conn, MS, Ed., Literacy specialist, Read-Ability, Inc.

Photo Credits: Cover and pages 1 and 25, ©guruXOX/Shutterstock; page 5, ©Robert Kneschke/Shutterstock; page 6, ©sculpies/Shutterstock; page 8, ©Dragon Images/Shutterstock; pages 11 and 16, ©Monkey Business Images/Shutterstock; page 12, ©Phovoir/Shutterstock; page 14, ©ALPA PROD/Shutterstock; page 15, ©topten22photo/Shutterstock; page 19, ©pikselstock/Shutterstock; page 20, ©SeventyFour/Shutterstock; page 22, ©Master1305/Shutterstock; page 26, ©Dusan Petkovic/Shutterstock; page 28, ©Tyler Olson/Shutterstock

Library of Congress Cataloging-in-Publication Data
Names: Mara, Wil, author.
Title: Be a carpenter / by Wil Mara.
Description: Ann Arbor, Michigan : Cherry Lake Publishing, [2019] | Series: 21st century skills library | Includes bibliographical references and index.
Identifiers: LCCN 2019003502| ISBN 9781534148222 (lib. bdg.) | ISBN 9781534149656 (pdf) | ISBN 9781534151086 (pbk.) | ISBN 9781534152519 (ebook)
Subjects: LCSH: Carpentry—Vocational guidance—Juvenile literature.
Classification: LCC TH5608.7 .M365 2019 | DDC 694.023—dc23
LC record available at https://lccn.loc.gov/2019003502

Cherry Lake Publishing would like to acknowledge the work of The Partnership for 21st Century Learning. Please visit *www.p21.org* for more information.

Printed in the United States of America
Corporate Graphics

ABOUT THE AUTHOR

Wil Mara is the author of over 175 fiction and nonfiction books for children. He has written many titles for Cherry Lake Publishing, including the popular *Global Citizens: Modern Media* and *Citizen's Guide* series. More about his work can be found at www.wilmara.com.

TABLE OF CONTENTS

CHAPTER 1

A Carpenter's Life

Professional carpenter Scott Preston shuts off the alarm at exactly 5:15 a.m. and gets out of bed. He takes a hot shower and gets dressed. Like he does on every other workday, he puts on jeans and heavy boots. He wears suspenders because they hold the jeans up better than a belt. He also has a jacket with a thick lining to keep him warm. He'll be working outside today, and the weather report says it will be chilly. He wishes it were a little warmer, but he still prefers the fresh air and sunshine to sitting behind a desk.

Breakfast is scrambled eggs, bacon, and coffee. Then Scott gets into his truck and hits the road. He loves his old truck.

[21ST CENTURY SKILLS LIBRARY]

Working as a carpenter often means early mornings and long days spent outdoors.

It has seen a lot of use over the years. Scott doesn't work for a big company like his wife does. He runs his own carpentry business, which means he works for himself. About one-third of all carpenters do this. Scott likes being his own boss. He gets to make a lot of important decisions, and he can set his own schedule.

The U.S. economy is growing, and that's good news for Scott and other carpenters. This means the number of

Watching the shape of a building appear as you work is one of the most satisfying parts of being a carpenter.

employed carpenters is also growing—by about 8 percent each year. Also, Scott lives in New Jersey, a state with many people in it. Heavily populated places like New Jersey are great for carpenters because there's lots of construction going on. Places with fewer people usually don't have as much new construction.

Scott arrives at the day's job **site**. It is a brand-new house that is being built from the ground up. The first thing Scott does is talk to the foreman. This is the person in charge of the entire building process. He and the foreman look over the **blueprints**, which show how the house needs to be put together. Then he goes back to his truck to get the tools he will need. These include power tools like a circular saw and a nail gun. Scott also uses simpler hand tools like a hammer and a utility knife.

Throughout the day, Scott measures and cuts pieces of wood to fit the needs of the blueprints. He carefully assembles the cut pieces to create the wooden skeleton of a house. The wood forms walls and ceilings, and the shape of the house starts to appear. Even though he's done jobs like this many times, Scott still feels proud every time he sees a project start to come together.

The day's work wraps up in late afternoon, and Scott heads home. He's got sawdust all over his clothes, so he brushes himself off before going inside. Then it's time for another shower. His muscles ache from the work, but it is a good, satisfying feeling.

A full day of sawing wood often leaves a carpenter covered in sawdust.

Scott has a quiet dinner with his family, watches a little TV, and heads off to bed. Tomorrow will be here soon enough. There's a lot more work to be done before that house can become someone's home.

21st Century Content

There are about 1 million carpenters employed in the United States each year. The states that employ the most are listed here:

California—97,000
New York—48,000
Florida—43,000
Texas—38,000
Pennsylvania—29,000

NOTE: These figures do not include self-employed carpenters.

CHAPTER 2

Becoming a Carpenter

An advanced college degree is not needed to become a carpenter. But that doesn't mean carpenters don't need any formal education. In fact, carpentry requires study and practice in some very specific subject areas.

Learning can begin as early as high school. Aside from the carpentry basics taught in shop class, subjects such as geometry, algebra, and physics will be helpful. Students can also develop important skills through art classes. Basic drawing, for example, will be part of any carpentry career.

After high school, students who want to become carpenters can consider a few different options for further education.

Many of the subjects a student takes in school, such as math and science, will help them get started with a career in carpentry.

Working with wood might seem simple at first, but there is a lot to learn before a beginning carpenter can start putting a house together.

Trade schools, vocational schools, and community colleges all offer courses with a focus on carpentry skills. Students in these classes will learn how to use and care for a variety of tools. They will also learn about job safety, how to read and understand blueprints, and more.

A carpentry student also needs to learn about the basics of building, such as **framing**, roofing, flooring, and **finishing**. There will be training in the latest construction technologies, which are advancing all the time. Another great advantage of attending carpentry classes is that students learn from experienced professionals. Teachers give real-time training where students are required to perform a variety of carpentry tasks on their own.

For students who are unable to travel, carpentry courses are available online through some schools. Students who have already received formal training can even benefit from online courses. It's an easy way to brush up on the basics or keep up with emerging techniques and technologies.

After getting an education, a young carpenter must go through on-the-job training. This can also be done instead of

Apprentices help more experienced workers complete real-life carpentry jobs. In return, they get useful on-the-job experience.

getting a formal education. Either way, for this training, an entry-level carpenter is usually paired with an experienced professional called a master carpenter. This kind of training is known as an **apprenticeship**. Apprentices are usually required to work for two to three years before they are qualified to do the job on their own.

Most of an apprentice's time is spent assisting the master carpenter. First lessons are often in safety and first aid. From there, the apprentice will sharpen his or her skills in

Safety is important in any construction job. Carpenters often wear brightly colored vests, hard hats, and other protective gear when they are at big job sites.

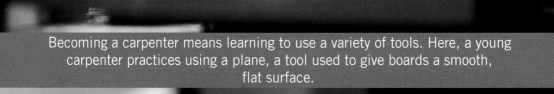

Becoming a carpenter means learning to use a variety of tools. Here, a young carpenter practices using a plane, a tool used to give boards a smooth, flat surface.

reading blueprints, making sketches, and performing basic carpentry duties. Then the apprentice will work at more advanced tasks such as framing and finishing on actual job sites. At the end of the apprenticeship, the student usually receives some type of formal certification and is then free to begin a carpentry career.

Life and Career Skills

There are generally three career categories within the field of carpentry. The first is called residential carpentry. This kind of work usually involves homes. It deals with the construction or remodeling of houses, condominiums, and apartments. The second is called commercial carpentry. It deals with the construction of structures such as offices, hotels, schools, and retail stores. Finally, there is industrial carpentry. A carpenter in this field will build things such as **scaffolding**, supports for bridges and tunnels, or concrete forms for massive structures such as dams and power plants.

CHAPTER 3

The Ups and Downs of Carpentry

Carpentry can be a very rewarding profession. Carpenters feel a tremendous sense of pride when driving past a new building or home they helped put up.

But carpentry can also be highly challenging. It is a very physical profession, which means a carpenter needs to stay in good shape. The average day can start early and last around eight to nine hours. While there will be breaks, most of that time will be spent in motion. Lifting materials or working power tools can be demanding on the body. But a carpenter who spends a lot of time sitting around probably won't get hired again.

Physical strength often comes in handy for carpenters.

Carpenters who run their own businesses must have good communication skills. They deal directly with clients, employees, and many other people every day.

Mistakes can be costly, so a carpenter's mind needs to be sharp as well. This isn't always easy, particularly on days that run longer than usual. There will be times when a carpenter needs to work many hours at a time. If a building plan changes at the last minute, the carpenter has to be able to adjust. If a job is being rushed in order to meet a deadline, the carpenter has to know how to hurry without sacrificing quality.

21st Century Content

It can be dangerous to work in construction, regardless of workers' attention to safety. Statistics suggest that every worker in the construction field is likely to suffer at least one workplace injury during their career.

More than 7 million people are employed each year in the U.S. construction industry. Of that number, nearly 1,000 workers are killed on the job each year. The most common cause of death is falling. Other risks include being struck by an object or receiving a severe electrical shock.

Protective glasses or goggles help protect a carpenter's eyes from sawdust and wood chips while using power saws.

Beyond these challenges, carpentry can also pose some real dangers. Among the most common are potential injuries to the eyes and ears. Over time, many carpenters suffer hearing loss from daily exposure to loud machinery. Power tools operate at high volumes and are often used for many hours for days on end. Eye injuries are also common. Eyes can be damaged by flying sawdust and wood chips. In addition, a carpenter will be exposed to a variety of chemicals. If they are not handled carefully, some can cause serious diseases.

Repetitive strain injuries are another hazard. These are caused by physical movements that must be repeated many times in order to perform certain tasks. For example, a carpenter may have to use a nail gun for hours at a time. The motion of firing nails from such a heavy device causes stress on certain parts of the body. Carpenters may also have to stand, sit, kneel, or lie in awkward positions for long periods.

In spite of all this, the rewards of the carpenter's trade can be quite good. The pay varies tremendously, from around $27,000 to $80,000 per year. The average salary is around $45,000. The exact pay per carpenter will depend on many factors, such as experience, difficulty of the job at hand, and location. A carpenter can join a **union**. Unions often negotiate for higher pay and other benefits, such as health insurance. Some jobs will offer the option of working overtime, which usually pays at a higher scale. This, however, requires giving up some weeknights, weekends, or even holidays.

CHAPTER 4

Rules and Regulations

Some states require professional carpenters to be **licensed** before they can work legally. The licensing requirements vary from state to state. In some cases, a carpenter has to have a certain number of hours of on-the-job experience, usually gained during their apprenticeship. Some states give tests to make sure a carpenter's skills and knowledge are at acceptable levels.

Often a carpenter cannot be officially licensed without also being **bonded**. This means the carpenter has purchased a bond that acts as a kind of insurance policy. If the carpenter causes damage during a job, the insurance will cover the costs

Experienced carpenters with a solid work record should have little trouble meeting the requirements to get bonded.

to repair it. Let's say a carpenter is remodeling a living room and has to knock down some old walls and pull up old floorboards. During this part of the project, the carpenter accidentally pierces a water pipe, sending water shooting out. This damages furniture and causes a small flood. The bond will cover the costs of this damage. A carpenter obviously hopes to never need the coverage provided by a bond. But there's a good chance something like this will eventually happen during the course of a carpentry career.

Being a carpenter isn't always about physical labor. It can also involve project planning, business management, and other office work.

Anyone looking to become a carpenter should be licensed and bonded even if their state doesn't require it. Doing these things will make it easier to get jobs. People prefer a carpenter who is licensed and bonded over one who isn't. They feel more

Life and Career Skills

Some basic business classes can give a carpenter career options beyond carpentry work itself. For example, anyone looking to start a carpentry company will benefit from learning about basic project management, building codes, and cost estimation.

Project management is important to anyone hoping to run a business. These people are in charge of everything, and the other workers will look to them for answers.

Building codes are rules set by a town, county, or state. They determine how different structures should be built. For example, a new home has to be a certain distance from a sidewalk, a road, or the other houses nearby.

Cost estimation is important because a carpenter has to know how much a job will cost before it's started. The carpenter must calculate the cost of supplies, labor, and any other expenses. That way, the client will get an accurate price for the work.

If you have an interest in buildings and how they are constructed, carpentry could be the perfect career for you.

certain that the quality of this carpenter's work and level of experience will be top notch. Any disagreement between a licensed carpenter and the person who hired them can be resolved by the state's licensing board. In addition, a carpenter who makes a costly mistake on the job but isn't bonded will personally have to pay the damages.

Becoming a licensed carpenter starts by making contact with a state's licensing board. This can usually be done online by going to the board's website, where the requirements are also posted. The carpenter will likely need to provide a list of past and present employers in order to show work experience. The test a carpenter eventually takes will cover general knowledge of the trade as well as business-related rules and regulations. The carpenter is usually not required to take classes in order to prepare for the test.

Obtaining a bond is based on several factors. One is the carpenter's yearly income. Another is the carpenter's work history. If the carpenter has already been sued for work-related issues, obtaining a bond will be much more difficult.

Think About It

Carpentry is one of the oldest professions in the world. Long before there were power tools—even back when hand tools were crudely made—humans were building homes and other structures. What kinds of materials do you think they used back then? And how did they go about cutting, connecting, and shaping them?

You can learn all about the different types of carpentry online. If you decide to be a carpenter, which area of the profession would you prefer? Would you like to build new homes? Or are you more interested in the delicate work of building cabinets or furniture? What would be your favorite aspects of this profession? What aspects do you think you wouldn't like? Why?

Find Out More

BOOKS

Hindman, Susan. *Carpenter.* Ann Arbor, MI: Cherry Lake Publishing, 2014.

Labrecque, Ellen. *Carpenter.* Ann Arbor, MI: Cherry Lake Publishing, 2016.

WEBSITES

Make—Ten Easy Woodworking Projects
https://makezine.com/2011/02/16/top-10-easy-woodworking-projects
Check out these woodworking projects for beginners. Ask an adult to help you
with one of them!

U.S. Bureau of Labor Statistics—Occupational Outlook Handbook: Carpenters
https://www.bls.gov/ooh/construction-and-extraction/carpenters.htm
Learn how to become a carpenter and more about the profession at this govern-
ment site.

GLOSSARY

apprenticeship (uh-PREN-tis-ship) training situation in which someone learns a skill by working with an expert on the job

blueprints (BLOO-printz) drawings that illustrate how a structure needs to be built

bonded (BAHND-id) having an insurance policy to cover damages caused by a worker while on the job

finishing (FIN-ih-shing) the final steps of a carpentry job, when everything is made to look nice

framing (FRAME-ing) building the supportive inner parts of a structure, such as the wooden studs behind a wall

licensed (LYE-suhnsd) receiving certification by the state that assures quality of service

repetitive strain (rih-PET-ih-tiv STRAYN) injury caused by performing the same motion over and over, or by positioning the body awkwardly for long periods

scaffolding (SKAF-uhl-ding) temporary structures used by workers to access high parts of a building during a job

site (SITE) the location of a carpentry job

union (YOON-yuhn) an organization that protects the interests of a certain type of worker, such as a carpenter

INDEX